FOR THE LOVE OF
PURPOSE

TAKE THESE
7 POWERFUL STEPS TO
ACHIEVE YOUR PURPOSE

CHIZUBEL EGWUDO

For The Love of Purpose: Take These 7 Powerful Steps to Achieve your Purpose.

First Edition

ISBN 978-1-8384349-1-5

The Editor was Mari Jones
The Designer was Jake J Bryant

To order copies for you or your team, go to
www.chizubelegwudo.com or call +44 (0)1908 464 420.

*FOR THE LOVE
OF ODEDRA AND ODETE,
MY DAUGHTERS*

EVERYTHING STARTS WITH A PURPOSE

CONTENTS

PREFACE

The consequence of having no clear purpose is a condition that leaves many in a state of helplessness and aimlessness. When you feel this way, frustration comes in and, when that happens, it can lead to all sorts of problems, health and psychological problems, money problems, family disruption and many more. In the world today, it is a dangerous thing for you not to have a clear purpose or not to have one at all. Throughout history, humans have been consumed with the quest for meaning. There have been great strides made by people and businesses to achieve many feats. Some have followed a pattern, while many dive in without any form of process in the hope that they will achieve something great. Why? Because it makes us feel good when we succeed.

Like many, you may have started out to achieve something great for yourself, a degree, a job, family or business, but never really thought that these achievements need to be in, or part of, a purpose. So many make this proverbial mistake of trying to build a house from the roof down instead of from the foundation up.

Everyone needs to start with a purpose, know what it is first, and then add the right elements to your purpose. There are more than 7.5 billion people on the planet earth today; have you wondered why only a handful are very successful? It is because billions of people do not have a purpose, or they have one, but it is not clearly defined. As a result, you miss out on the rewards a defined purpose brings. You allow your share of success to be taken by the very few who control the wealth on the earth today. They have actually taken the time to define their purpose and you can't blame them for having more. This successful few are having a windfall and taking more of the market share than they can handle.

Imagine if we were all educated correctly at school, from a young age, with purpose as the foundational doctrine where you are taught what purpose is, how to define yours, and you are helped with the steps to achieve it.

There would be an equilibrium of wealth on earth, no poverty. Unfortunately, this is not the case. Know this, every single person on this planet today has something to offer to a fraction of the world's population and would not need to suffer or beg for food. But you must follow the right process.

In this book, I show you the process and the strategies you can use to achieve your purpose. What you get in this book is wisdom that can transform your life. I want to help you and millions of other people by sharing these vital steps that are working for me to help you achieve your purpose. The important information I give you in this book forms part of the fulfilment of my own purpose. That is why I am on a mission to help people around the world use the system I created in this book, to achieve their own successes.

It is my mission to have this book translated into several languages for it to reach as many people as possible.

This book is my introduction as a long-time writer and author of more books to come.

Please enjoy reading this simple, straightforward and applicable book, and use it as a guide to help you to achieve your purpose.

INTRODUCTION

As suggested by the title of this book, ***this is a demand I am making to you to make your purpose a priority.*** This includes defining what your purpose is, and having a clear roadmap to getting to your purpose and beyond. This is different for each person and each organisation. Making your purpose come true is not an illusion. You can make your purpose real. It does not matter where you are in the world, whether you come from a poor background or a rich one, or what racial category you come under, whether you live in the slums, city or suburbs; you can be successful in life by making your purpose come true. Sometimes people say, "I want to be rich", "I want to be famous", "I want this house by the beach" or "that fast car". Nothing wrong with wanting these things, but the question you must ask yourself is, "what purpose will this be fulfilling?" Thought without purpose is like going hunting, and shooting at trees in the forest instead of the beast you came hunting for. You will never bring home the kill for dinner. What a waste of ammunition that will be. Your thoughts are like ammunition you have to aim them in the direction of your purpose.

Mental deficit, or what I call non-functional illiteracy, where a person lacks the intellectual capacity to make common-sense decisions due to self-imposed ignorance, prevents one from conscious learning that is aligned with the achievement of a defined purpose.

In this book you will get a clear understanding of what purpose is. It has clear methods designed to help you achieve your purpose. I will show you in seven practical steps how you can achieve the purpose you define for yourself which many of the other books have not done. I will also show you how you can use failure to your advantage. These are the steps I am using to successfully achieve my own purpose beyond that which I could ever imagine, and also helping my family and clients achieve theirs.

Like many of you reading this book, I come from a middle-class family and it took me a few years to understand what my purpose is; not until after several failed events in my life, from failed businesses to failed relationships and personal ambitions. What I came to realise from these failures was that I was not comfortable with mediocrity of any sort. When I started to take steps to define and execute my purpose, the things I never thought were possible became achievable. Why? Because I now know how, and it is that 'HOW' I am sharing with you in this book. You have to do as I did, and ask yourself these questions: *What is my purpose? What opportunity is my failure presenting to me? Why do I struggle to have the vital resources I need in life, such as money? What can I do to have more money to meet the increasing cost of living? What sort of people do I need to have in my life to achieve my purpose? How do I start from nothing to achieving my purpose successfully?* My mind raced on thoughts like these. I wasn't thinking about the money, the cars or the things money can buy, but I began to see that, to get anywhere near or beyond some of the successes of the very wealthy, you have to have a purpose, and follow that purpose with the right process and people. I understood that beyond the wealth there is something greater. I understood that my purpose has to fit into a greater purpose, Universal Purpose. Chapter Seven in particular talks about this in more detail.

What I share with you in this book are seven simple, valuable steps that are helping me, and that have helped many people, achieve the successes they have today. Who is your favourite successful person or someone you admire that is very wealthy? I mean, someone who really worked for their wealth not those who got it from corrupt, illegal means or inheritance. Someone with virtue. That person may have followed most, if not all, of these steps to achieve their success.

Now let's do the same for you. Begin with Step One now.

I

Step One: Define Your Purpose

You have to define your purpose on a personal level first before you can do this in your business or in any other initiative you want to start in life. It doesn't matter what your religious affiliation is, or what you believe. On the grand scale of the universe, you are here for a reason. This is the fundamental aspect we most often do not take note of. For you to get into the production state you need to be in to create a purposeful and worthy life, you need to affirm within yourself that you know your purpose. As you can see, I didn't say that you have to know the reason that you are put in the universe because, for most people, that is a mystery. The thing is that you know you are here, and you have control over the path you define for yourself, and this is what I want to focus on - the defining of your purpose which gives reason to your existence and everything that comes from it.

Why is that so important? It is important because it means your life. The value of your purpose determines whether you have that life or not. Becoming who I am today has come from learning from my failures and successes. Putting all that conscious and unconscious learning into refining my purpose has given me clarity and the determination to see more opportunities to bring my purpose to fruition. This would not happen if my purpose and the path to it was not clearly mapped out.

Like most people, you likely set goals, make plans or have New Year resolutions. While that may be with the best intentions, it is widely known that most people do not achieve what they set out to. According to a research carried out by the University of Scranton in Pennsylvania USA, 92% of people who set goals every year don't achieve them. That is a huge number, and I was at one time in that category of people who set goals and don't get to achieve them, until I got to understand that goals on their own are not enough. You can set goals all you want but, without your goals being in an entity, you would likely not achieve them satisfactorily. You have to give your goals a home to live in and that home is **<u>PURPOSE</u>**. Why do you buy clothes to wear? Because you have a body to put them on. Why do you buy a piece of furniture? Because you have a home to put it in. In a similar way, goals need a place to be put in like that piece of furniture. On their own, your goals will likely not survive.

The moment I realised I needed to clearly define my purpose and then use goals to support the purpose, my goals became fully operational. It is like turning on the ignition of a car in order for it to take you to your destination. Whether it is in your personal life or business, you have to align your goals with your purpose. Once you do that, the result will be like a miracle, the pathway to your success will become much clearer and start to align better. But you have to understand what purpose is.

The Meaning of Purpose

Purpose is simply the reason for something or someone's existence. It answers the questions: *Why am I here? What am I living for? What value do I offer? How do I make my life and the life of others better? Is there a global good to my existence?* The 'I' in these questions refers to you as a person or an entity such as an organisation or a business, whether small or large. The answer to these questions will go a long way to helping you define your purpose.

We all have a reason for why we exist, why we study a subject, why we set up businesses or become entrepreneurs. The question of "why this?" or "why that?" needs to be answered first before setting the goals to achieve that "why".

As a risk strategist, I find purpose in everything I do as a result of my purpose-driven analytical approach to bringing meaning to my life and the lives of clients I work with. My aim is to maintain definiteness of purpose. You need to do the same by gifting meaning to your life through definiteness of purpose.

Let's make your reason for existence meaningful by defining your purpose now!

The first thing you want to do now is to clearly work out what your purpose is. What is your purpose as a person? If you are in pursuit of a certain career, that purpose may have already been defined for you. For example, if you wanted to become a medical doctor, the purpose of being a doctor is to provide good healthcare and save lives. But you, as the individual, need to define your purpose in relation to the purpose of being a medical doctor.

All businesses have a purpose, whether small ones or big ones. You can't set up or run a business without a purpose and expect it to flourish. Many businesses, especially small ones, are set up without a clear purpose or none at all. There are many people who start businesses because they are looking for a side hustle, as it is often referred to. Some do this with the aim of supplementing income from their employment jobs, whilst others are trying out an idea to see if it will work. The problem with this kind of approach or similar is that it is not driven by real commitment and a clear purpose.

This is also true for many individuals who want to start a business but are too afraid to leave the safety net of their employment. It is like being torn between two lovers. You don't make any real progress with either. I did that in the past when I was a novice in business, and I'm not in business with any of those ideas because there was no purpose to them. If you really want to be successful in business, or anything else, you have to go all in.

To determine your purpose, you have to take a deep look into yourself to identify your abilities, skills, experiences, likes, dislikes, emotional agility level, mental capability, health and wellbeing. This basic internal self-assessment will help you to work out your purpose and align yourself with it. By carrying out this self-examination after I had made some mistakes in the early years of my life, I was able to define my purpose in life more clearly and took the appropriate steps I am sharing with you in this book, to achieve it.

Synergy between person and business or career is very important. If you are disconnected from the purpose of your business or career, you will not succeed. Synergy makes purpose evident. Your business purpose needs to be clearly defined; what is its reason for existence? It is only when you define the purpose of your business that you can visualise it. The visualisation of your purpose is like seeing the finish line in a difficult race. You keep going, using every fibre of strength in your body, despite the pain, because you know it is achievable. This vision keeps you accountable when no one else believes in you or your dreams.

If you are just realising the need to define your purpose, or understanding that you need goals to facilitate your purpose, don't worry; it is not too late. All you have to do now is carry out some realignment, define your purpose then align the goals to the purpose. Remember, *goals do not stand alone, they belong in a purpose.*

When I work with clients who have been running their businesses for several years, who want to strategise or realign, the first thing I do with them is to clarify, or help them define, the purpose of the business. Most of the clients I have worked with did not have their business purpose clearly defined. They have business plans, corporate goals, missions which were not integrated with purpose. Purpose consists of integrated elements.

I take the people I work with through this process that I am now going to share with you and by the end of the session, they were singing **do-re-mi-fa-so-la-ti-do** all the way forward to success. Hopefully, you can sing along when you follow this simple process to your success.

First and very important! Never set goals on their own. Ask yourself, what purpose is the goal I am about to set supporting? Your goals should be supporting your purpose.

Secondly, you have to do these 4 things:

- Define your purpose.
- Visualise the channel by which your purpose is realised. This means that you have to design and develop it.
- Identify the things, or people, you need to accomplish your purpose.
- Set purposeful goals – I will talk exclusively about goals in Chapter 2.

Follow the process and read every chapter in this book

progressively. There is a process for everything in the universe and most times the human in us wants to skip the steps in the process and get to the result faster. The problem with that is we don't learn the fundamentals of life or business. Worse yet, you learn the hard way, as I did. The only thing you want to skip, if possible, is learning life and business the hard way. Follow the process to achieving your purpose and it will bring you much more joy than pain when you see the rewarding results becoming more and more real. Nothing happens for nothing. See purpose in everything, work on your purpose, help others achieve their purpose but make sure that whatever purpose you latch onto aligns with your own purpose and helps you achieve your purpose. It is not being selfish; it is being intentional and meaningful.

The 5 Pillars of Purpose

There are 5 pillars of purpose and they are: Vision, Objectives, Roadmap, Mission and Strategy. They flow in this exact order. If you want to represent this mathematically, the formula is:

$$P(Purpose) = V(Vision) + O(Objectives) +$$
$$R(Roadmap) + M(Mission) + S(Strategy)$$

Description of the 5 Pillars of Purpose

1. **Vision:** This is what you see your purpose becoming, or the channel by which your purpose is fulfilled. *If your purpose is to be a maths teacher, then the **vision** through which that is fulfilled is by **you teaching in a classroom** after going through the appropriate channel designed for you to become a maths teacher. You can't be a teacher by that thought living in your brain for the rest of your life. Another possible channel or vision through which the purpose of being a maths teacher can be fulfilled is by you having your own online maths teaching platform, giving afterschool private maths lessons or owning your own school. Whatever is possible.* Try not to think traditionally or follow traditional patterns set. The world has advanced so much and you need to adapt if you are to thrive. Following traditional patterns limits your options of what is possible and pits you against thousands of other people vying for the same thing. It also reduces your bargaining power.

2. **Objectives:** These are the things you need to achieve your purpose. *Continuing with the maths teacher example, what do you need to be a maths teacher? The desire, and passion for the profession would help, money to pay for the teacher training qualification, practice, maths textbooks, etc.*

3. **Roadmap:** This is the trusted guide or map you need, with executable goals and outputs to achieve your purpose. You will be using your objectives and strategy to execute your roadmap. *As a maths teacher to be, you need to draw up a roadmap which includes your timeline, goals and milestones. I use the project management term of milestone, which is simply the start to end of a phase. The end of the phase is the definite part of that phase and marks the beginning of the next. It indicates progression to the purpose as the goals of that phase are complete. Milestones act as markers in your roadmap.*

Let's use the diagram on the next page as an example to illustrate this, on the assumption that the time it takes you to achieve this purpose is 12 months:

ROADMAP DIAGRAM

12 MONTH TIMELINE

Milestone/Phase 1 - End of Month 1

GOALS

1. *Get advice from other maths teachers.*
2. *Register for maths teacher training programme.*

Milestone/Phase 2 - End of Month 3

GOALS

1. *Commence maths teacher training programme.*
2. *Join a maths teachers' association or professional body.*

Milestone/Phase 3 - End of Month 6

GOALS

1. *Apply for Teaching Assistant Position in school.*
2. *Work as a Teaching Assistant.*

Milestone/Phase 4 - End of Month 9

GOALS

1. *Prepare for Final Exams.*
2. *Take all Final Exams.*

Milestone/Phase 5 - End of Month 12

GOALS

1. *Apply for Qualified Teacher Jobs.*
2. *Work as a Qualified Teacher.*

Create a roadmap for every purpose, whether it is a business purpose, a professional purpose, or a personal purpose. The timeline for a roadmap can vary in length, from 12 months to 100 years if you want to leave a legacy. For countries, the roadmap needs to exceed 100 years. Legacy builders think beyond 50 years. When the pioneers of the legacies are gone, their legacy lives on through the things they created.

4. **Mission:** This is the offering, output, product, or service of your purpose which brings value to the desired audience or beneficiaries. In the case of a business, it is products or services. Every business is on a mission to deliver its product or service. *As a maths teacher, your main offering (mission) or service is your skill as a maths teacher. This can extend to products such as authoring maths books, calculation tools or maths e-learning platform.*

5. **Strategy:** This is the continuous system of approach that keeps your purpose functional. You need to establish this system, adjust it, adapt it, and maintain it throughout the course of your purpose. It is your holistic and dynamic risk assessment that becomes habit. *To*

keep your purpose functional as a maths teacher, you have to have a continuous system of approach. A great way to do that is to maintain membership with maths teachers' professional associations.

Let's take this a notch up and use a simple example to demonstrate how you can use the **5 Pillars of Purpose** together as a framework for anything you want to achieve, whether it's in business or in your personal life. I am going to use marriage as the example since most people can relate to it.

Purpose – *Purpose Defined:*
To be the quintessence of true love in marriage until death do you part.

Vision – *Visualise how it becomes real:*
The first date, courtship, the wedding, and the marriage entity.

Objectives – *Outline the things you need:*
You need respect, love, intimacy, patience, faithfulness, thoughtfulness, kindness, dutifulness, affection, loyalty, leadership, income, health and fitness, communication,

etc. One minister illustrated marriage as an empty box into which you bring all these elements. If you as an individual don't have it, and you get into marriage, the purpose of marriage will not be achieved. It is the same with any other purpose whether personal or professional. You simply cannot put the valuable elements into your defined purpose if you haven't developed them. Give to yourself first before you can give to your purpose. This means personal development on all fronts of your life which will influence everything you do and become. *Note, for organisations or businesses, this will include your governance structure, the people, skills, capital, operations, and everything required to facilitate your purpose.*

Roadmap – *Your trusted guide as mentioned in the explanation above, which gets you to your purpose.* Remember those goals we talked about? List the short-term, midterm and long-term goals. They play a very important role. You want to set long-term goals that will outlive the wedding. Your roadmap needs to be in phases with milestones along a timeline. The average marriage timeline in the United Kingdom, according to the Office for National Statistics (ONS), before the death of a spouse, is 40 years. Let's try this:

- **Year 1:** build deep and complex levels of closeness, build on family business. Holiday to two countries.
- **Year 5:** have two children, buy a home with a stable in the countryside, increase network and engage with other successful couples and families. Holiday to 5 new countries.
- **Year 7:** learn new languages, co-author a book. Relocate to another country. Holiday to 2 new countries
- **Year 15 and beyond:** engage and support in community development works, explore the world as a couple and family. Increase net worth financial value. Trust fund for children. Post life planning, etc.

The year markers here indicate the milestone point as previously explained in No. 3 of Pillar 5. Use the example in the diagram above to draw up a comprehensive roadmap. For every business, you should have a minimum of a 25-year timeline in your roadmap with succession planning goals included. Your roadmap can be as granular as you want it. Here is a flightpath you may consider:

Roadmap ‣ Milestones ‣ Goals ‣ Targets ‣ Tasks

You know what a roadmap is. You now know clearly how to structure your goals. Take note, targets form part of your milestone; they are shorter timelines of tasks you wish to achieve within one day and one week. These tasks bring quick incremental value that contributes to the achievement of your purpose.

Mission – *The offer to your audience, beneficiaries (products and services):*
What is the typical product and service of most marriages?

- Have children is usually number one.
- Entertain family and friends through regular events.

Strategy – *The continuous system of approach that keeps the marriage functional*
Strategy is 360 degrees. It is continuous, adaptive, flexible, and advanced. It is applied 24 hours a day, 7 days a week and 365 days of the year, including a leap year when that applies. No days off. The day you take off could be the day you create an opening for problems.

Some examples of strategic activities to have in place include:

- Risk Assessment *(includes threats, problems, opportunities and rewards)*
- Communication
- Transparency
- Spirituality
- Family Meetings
- Regular Mealtimes
- Recreation
- Entertainment
- Problem Management

Using marriage as an illustration, I demonstrated how you can use the 5 Pillars of Purpose framework for the achievement of any purpose you want to achieve in life or business. Now take your defined purpose and use the 5 Pillars of Purpose to frame it. Map it all out. This will help you to bring your defined purpose to reality with assured success.

I urge you to define your purpose and be definite about it by backing it up with a roadmap. Your purpose does not change if you experience any apparent roadblock or failure. Adapt and stay focused. Be definite about your purpose, both in your thoughts and actions. This will lead you to achieve your purpose successfully. It is the law and dynamics of life. You get out what you put in. No film tricks, no juju, no magic. Just simple dynamics.

Try This

1. Write down your purpose in two forms: A personal one and a secular one (in any professional sense, whether business, employment or other).

2. Through what channel will your purpose become real? This is your visualisation. Pin it down to one thing for starters. Once you have mastered it, then you can expand to other purpose.

3. Identify the things you need to achieve your purpose and bring them together to begin work. Include personal.

4. Never let a day go by without you purposefully completing an activity that incrementally brings you

closer to your purpose no matter how small.

5. If you have achieved your purpose, be aware of the events that may happen which could derail it and then adapt your strategy to keep your purpose relevant. This is part of your risk assessment.

II

Step Two: Create A Roadmap For Your Purpose

We talked a bit about a roadmap in Chapter 1. Let's build on that. When you are clear on what your purpose is, whether it is a personal one or business, and you have visualised it, you need a roadmap to get you there. It is like seeing the top of Mount Everest from the ground with the intention of getting to the top. You need to follow one of the climbing routes, guided by a map, to navigate your way to the top. You just can't walk up in any direction and expect to get to the top. You might end up dead, like many have. It is a dangerous thing as well to try to navigate life or business without a trusted guide. Your roadmap contains the essential ingredients for your success. These are your goals and mission.

Goals are the output of a defined activity that

produces a desired outcome. This desired outcome is your mission, the value offer *(that is, the output of your purpose)* that you use to satisfy or solve the needs and wants of your active and passive audience such as your family, friends, peers, customers, clients or community. Your mission in life is to fulfil the purpose of others. The satisfaction of the needs and wants of your active and passive audience is an indication that you are fulfilling your purpose. By successfully doing so, you achieve the purpose you have defined. In other words, you effectively answer the aforementioned questions I outlined in Chapter 1. This allows the people you deal with to have confidence and trust in you. Without these components in your roadmap, achieving your purpose will be impossible, leaving you unfulfilled. That feeling of not being fulfilled is what leads many to give up on their dreams and aspirations.

As I mentioned in Chapter 1, goals do not stand alone. They live within a roadmap and keep you on the road to your purpose.

Think about your roadmap as a travel guide, just like satellite navigation systems or old-school paper maps. Imagine you are a delivery truck driver tasked with delivering five of the latest Range Rover SUVs to five eagerly waiting customers, between London and Edinburgh by road. You'd mainly be travelling up the M1 motorway. Along the way, you have what are called motorway junctions or highway interchanges, where two or more roads meet. These junctions are numbered progressively along the motorway; Junction one, Junction two, Junction three…Junction 31 until the end. Take London as the start of your roadmap, where you begin your journey, and Edinburgh as where you would have completed that journey or achieved that purpose to have all vehicles delivered. Each junction you pass through represents the goals along the way, and each one you successfully and progressively pass brings you closer to that purpose. There are several activities that take place during that journey; you stop to refuel your vehicle, use the restrooms, or get some food. As you deliver each vehicle to its owner, you progressively complete the goals of the purpose to deliver all five vehicles to their owners. Not four or three or two of them, but all five of the vehicles. That purpose is not fulfilled if, for some reason, such as being involved in an accident, you don't deliver all five vehicles, because it is only after you have delivered all five that you gain the reward of the purpose. You get fully paid. You increase your credibility and trustworthiness which leads to more opportunities and their eventual reward.

When you understand the concept of integrating goals into roadmaps, as I have shown you in this example and the ones in chapter 1, by applying it in anything you do, you will have fewer unrealised goals. You solve the common problem of unrealised goals that most people have because their goals are largely stand-alone and not built into a roadmap. Goals don't live independently; they live within the community of a roadmap in the same way that various organ cells live in your body. They do not live independently; cells live amongst the community of other cells in order for them to fulfil the purpose of you being a human being. Goals work in a similar manner.

The set of values associated with purpose consists of trust, honesty, commitment, determination, truthfulness, reliability, and other virtuous qualities. I call them your internal elements, the moral values that compel you to do the things you do. People often forget that you are first a person before anything else. People make up homes, schools, communities, companies or businesses and these institutions consist of all sorts of people with various internal elements (emotional, mental, physical and spiritual). If your internal elements, including those of the people in your inner circle, do not align with your purpose, your roadmap will be like a faulty navigation system or a map that's shrivelled up. You will get lost or stranded on the journey to your purpose.

Always draw up your roadmap in long terms, not short-term. Most businesses jump to setting short-term goals and fail to put their goals into a roadmap. That is why, when crisis happens, they are more likely to go out of business. When I work with clients and go through this exercise, we create roadmaps with batches of goals set for Year 1, 3, 7, 10 and above. I did this with a client in the property business who came to me for help and I took them through the process of building a purpose map for their business. Although they were doing okay, I identified that there were so many opportunities not being explored and they had huge potential to be a leading influencer in the UK property market. The problem was that they didn't have goals set for the long term. They were comfortable just getting by. I did my work on them and saw the many opportunities they were leaving unexploited, with many cracks which could lead to losses. I valued the business could be worth £500,000,000 in 10 years. They were astonished and didn't see how that was possible. But when I worked out and demonstrated, step by step, how they could exploit their opportunities, the £500,000,000 became a small number. It was more achievable because I helped them develop goals with money attached to it to create the roadmap to that £500,000,000. This involved lots of maths calculation in the forecast. If you don't add some kind of value or money incentive to your goals, your approach will be lacklustre.

Stop wasting time writing business plans and build a complete purpose map using the formula in chapter 1 with a value-driven roadmap. You'll be buzzing your way to your purpose, no matter the storm that rocks your boat. This powerful step leads to success, not just in business, but in every aspect of life.

Try This

1. Create a one-year roadmap with goals of a purpose in your personal life or business that you want to achieve using the method I have just shared with you. Think about it and follow the steps above.

2. Keep your end purpose in mind all the way.

3. Identify who and what you need to execute this roadmap.

4. Test it for the first month and see if it brings you closer to your purpose.

5. Tweak it if you need to.

III

Step Three: Educate Yourself The Right Way

Most people think education is about going to school or getting a degree. That can be useful, but the best education you can get comes from the University of Life and everyone is admitted into this great university from birth. I have had two university educations and neither of those is playing a part in my life or business today. They were basically a waste of time and, if I knew what I know now, I would have taken a different route earlier to get me to where I am now, quicker and much earlier.

Don't screw up your life getting a university education because your parents want that for you or it's some sort of status symbol. If you are not planning on becoming a medical doctor, lawyer or scientist, then I think you should reconsider any idea of taking up university education because you are more guaranteed accumulated debt than you are guaranteed a job in your field of study. Most very successful entrepreneurs will tell you that university education is not necessary for success. When you know your purpose, then you can learn what you need to do to achieve it and more. It is crazy that the current education systems don't teach you the order of learning. **Define your purpose – learn in accordance with your purpose – create your own success.** This order is what you should follow to learn what you need to learn in relation to your purpose.

People who don't find learning appealing do so because what they are learning feels like a chore and has little meaning for them. As a child, mandated learning was never exciting because there was no real meaning for me. I felt like I had to learn and pass exams to make my parents feel proud, not of me, but as bragging rights for themselves. I didn't even feel that good about myself the times I did well in school. But as I made learning more purposeful, I began to enjoy it because I was beginning to associate what I learnt with where I wanted to be in the future.

Just like me, you may come from a background or family that values the traditional education system and the alternatives, such as vocational or apprenticeship, were not looked on favourably. Whatever the case may be, do not let family, culture or tradition be your default learning factor, because how your life turns out will be the result of that decision. I wanted to be a chef with the intention of owning multiple restaurants. I couldn't bring myself to tell my parents that because I knew what the answer would be. Who knows what that would have led to? I ended up doing the university thing, like everyone else, which restricted my mental creative abilities to develop that thought to where it could have taken me.

Let me share 10 things with you that I have learned about learning that is helping me now progress on the road to my purpose successfully:

1. Learn purposefully to create your desired outcome

When I realised that my university education was not going to serve me in the way that I had envisioned my life, I ended it. Before I did, I had to battle with the thought of not having a degree. It is hard when everyone around you aims for that degree, even though more than 50% of the people who have degrees don't use what they have learned. What helped me overcome that mindset was the outcome of the lives of most university graduates that I know and have encountered through life. Many struggled to find work, and most ended up in work that was less dignifying, considering the course they studied and how much they had spent on their education. I didn't want to end up like them. More so, no university education would give me the kind of life and freedom I desired. This helped me make my decision not to pursue learning through the traditional method beyond the compulsory education years. From a young age, I always wanted to be my own boss, run my own business. So, what I did was channel my learning path along the lines of the outcome I wanted. I took practical courses that taught me what I needed to learn to work in the areas I did, which led me to have the skills that I have and to eventually establish my growing businesses. And my learning continues to this day, where I need to learn and take courses to help me achieve success in the areas of my life that I want to enhance to serve my purpose. Learning purposefully is satisfying and leads to a better outcome.

2. Learn from the people who can teach you the things you need to learn to help you get to where you want to go

This is very important because most times we get information or listen to people who cannot propel us to success or massive success. Grant Cardone, who I have also learned from, always says, "be careful where you get your advice from." You can't learn to be successful from someone who has no purpose and is not successful. Learning is contagious so choose to learn from people who are higher than you in the area of success you want to achieve. Find a mentor who is dynamic so that, even if you don't have a clear direction of where you want to go in life, they can reason with you and help you get there. They will help you grow and also keep you accountable. If you can't afford a paid mentor, adopt a virtual one with a proven system of work. Learn from them and adapt what they are doing for success to what you want to achieve. Don't forget to say thank you to them somehow, even though they may never meet you. Showing gratitude somehow has a way of paying you back.

3. Learning is not about information overload

You don't need to read every bit of literature out there. It is dangerous to your mind, also, to allow all forms of information to be absorbed. There is so much noise out there in the world right now that is readily available at our fingertips through our mobile devices. Social media is full of so much variety that you can find yourself surfing on end. My view is, if it is not serving you, it is hurting you. Be intentional about the information you take in through whatever channels. Every bit of wasted time never comes back to you so make it count.

4. Your life is your data

It is interesting what people say when I encourage them to write a book. The common one is, "what will I write about?" Now this is the time when you have to look inside the box and not outside. Start with you. Here is an "ah-ha!" moment – by the time you are an adult, you would have generated over 1 Terabyte (1TB) of data, and I am not talking Internet of Things data. I mean data in your thoughts; your thought is data, your experiences whether good or bad, what you see, feel, taste, smell, hear, emotional, physical, mental, spiritual. Translate this and you have about 6.5 million pages of document and you tell me you cannot write a book when all this data is stored inside of you? Use the data your life has given you; it will be a waste if you don't do some good with it. The reason why Google is so successful today is because of the amount of data it has collected. That is why you can type pretty much anything, in almost any language, in Google and get the resulting data you requested and more. Use your data wisely. Better still, monetise your data.

5. Psychological Intelligence is your closest teacher

Your mental and emotional wellness says a lot about how you learn. Research shows that when there are heightened triggers present in our lives, such as stress from external factors or health issues, learning can be difficult. It'll probably be difficult to pick up a book to learn something new. But ask yourself, what is your mental and emotional state teaching you? Who or what has triggered it? How did you respond to it? How did the people around you treat you during times of emotional or mental dilemmas? What did you do to take care of your psychological wellbeing and bring it into balance so you can be productive and creative? When I went through a very messy divorce in 2015 that wiped me out financially for the next two years, I was put under extreme stress psychologically, not primarily because of the money, but because my daughters were affected by this too. The long-drawn-out court appearances, not having the support of family or that of the friends who drifted away. I learned to focus on what was important, and that was me. You can call it self-centredness if you want, but it was essential that I maintained myself in order to tune out the noise from within me and outside. I had to redefine my purpose and push myself to learn new ways to approach life. When my vision became clearer, the path to my purpose presented itself to me, and today I am able to share a little bit of that with you.

6. "Oops!... I did it again." Grow from mistakes

Dan Clarke, author of the book, 'The Art of Significance – Achieving the Level Beyond Success' said, "pain is a signal to grow and not to suffer. When you learn the lessons pain teaches, in life there are no more mistakes but lessons." I could just stop there because that quote is so profound that it is embedded in my soul. Forgive yourself for the mistakes you have made, whether they are massive mistakes or tiny ones. Forgive yourself, and learn from them, because you will be a master at the things you learn from the mistakes you make. The conviction you have from them will fuel you to become successful in the purpose you define for yourself. I used both the less serious and more serious mistakes I have made in life to adapt the processes to my purpose. When you become a master at this, you see failure as raw gems ready to be refined, and high value is placed on the outcome. Let's talk about this more in Chapter 6.

7. Practise, practise, practise, what you learn

I often wonder where thoughts go to when I think them. If they are not used, and used repetitively, they disappear to wherever they go. I'm sure there is a perfectly good answer for that, but for now it is, "use it or lose it." The simplest way you can practise is by teaching what you learn. It creates positive patterns in your brain that retains the information you need to achieve your purpose. You have to challenge yourself to practise what you learn. Discomforting yourself, to put yourself in situations that will get you to embed what you learn, will pay massive dividends. Just walk up to someone and start teaching them what you know, or parts of it. They may think you are crazy but that's okay because the good result that comes from it is yours to keep. Join a club where you can share your expertise, help small businesses grow with what you know – do it for free or get paid for it, talk to family, friends, co-workers. Just practise. There is no other way. What can you do today to practise what you learn?

8. Evolve your brain

You possess so much power in your brain. We don't use the fraction of what we do use enough. We don't stretch it enough, and that failure to use the plasticity of our brains can be the difference between colossal failure or exponential success. It can be the difference between achieving your purpose through the goals you define or just getting by in life. You can extend your brain's plasticity just like an elastic band. Your brain's function, and effectively you as a person, does not grow when you don't do things at a progressive intensity level. It is like exercising or trying to achieve a certain fit body goal. If you don't increase the intensity of your workouts, and you repeat the same exercises every day, you will plateau. In the same way, you can't override genetically embedded patterns and rewire them for new functions if you don't exercise your brain by learning dynamically. The external prompt your brain receives and processes needs to be able to exert enough force to create change in you. In non-scientific words, your brain can take any information you give it, and you can also override strongly entrenched limitations that inhibit new learning. Don't feed your brain garbage because it will absorb it. Your brain does not control you as many people think; you control your brain. What you put in is what you get out of it. Don't overexpose your brain to disadvantageous information and experiences. Extended use of mind-altering substances and activities such as meaningless media consumption or drugs can limit the ability of your brain to be creative in relation to your purpose.

9. Identify your limitations to learning

If you really want to achieve a purposeful outcome in your life or business, identify the things and people that hinder your opportunity to learn the things you need to learn to achieve success for you, your family, and your contribution to the greater good of your community. Don't be afraid or shy to seek advice or guidance from people you can learn from. Take the approach that there is no such thing as a stupid question. Whatever answer you get from people will teach you something about yourself, the people you seek advice from, and the answers you get which will inform your actions.

10. Believe these undeniable truths about learning

You won't grow if you don't learn. You won't be happy if you don't learn. You won't be successful if you don't learn. You won't achieve a worthy purpose if you don't learn. You will be a burden to yourself and family if you don't learn. You learn every day because your brain takes in information whether you like it or not. Making what you learn more intentional than passive will make you more valuable and create more value in your life. To take it a step further, when you align your learning to your purpose, this can have a phenomenal effect in your life.

Try This

Just follow the ten steps above.

IV

Step Four: Understand How the World Works

You need to understand how the world works in relation to your purpose. There is a greater order of how things work in our society and, depending on where you want to place yourself, you need to understand the environment around the direction of travel for what you want to achieve. What is responsible for success? Who may be an obstacle? What are the regulations governing my products or service? Is there an appetite for my offering? What are the red tapes I have to know? Who are the people worth knowing? There are many more of these questions, including deeper ones, that need to be understood on a personal level as well, depending on how big an impact you want to make.

Most people choose to stay at a mediocre level because

they can't be bothered to overcome some of these objections. But if you want to achieve your purpose, you need to know that your purpose is not limited within your home or where you live. It is important for you to know that, for your purpose to have full success, you need to understand how its elements come together and work in unison for it to be achieved. I know it may sound like a lot to think about, but what is interesting is that, once you start to work on your purpose, the elements start to come together; they don't do so by chance. Imagine what can happen when you become more intentional about the actions you take to achieve your purpose. The results will be phenomenal! It is the reason why there are fewer very successful people; they are more intentional about the things they do and the elements that affect their purpose, and not leaving things to chance. This distinguishes them from the 'not-successful'. The interesting thing about the 'not-successful' group of people is that most of them want to be successful but they don't exert themselves hard enough to do the things required for that success.

Sadly, the people at the poverty line suffer the most because they do not know how, or have the knowledge they need, to provide for themselves and their families. What may surprise you is that there have been individuals who are in poverty, but not in 'poverty mentality', who have changed their life remarkably by aligning their thought with a greater purpose. Their thoughts were not constrained by 'poverty mentality.' You may have heard of the Slumdog Millionaire story; the movie is great, but I'm talking about the real-life version. This proves that the achievement of your purpose is not limited by the situation that you are placed in which you had no control over, like where you are born. It is your choice whether this holds you back from achieving your purpose or not. It was part of your parents' purpose to give birth to you where they did, but it is your responsibility to define and achieve your purpose in line with where you want to be beyond your parents' purpose.

Most people in the middle class don't aspire high enough. They mainly serve the interests of the few upper-class rich people. What we have is a disequilibrium of the vital information that is required to inform you on how to achieve your purpose. I am not talking about going to school, or university education, because you most likely will not acquire that vital information from secular education to be at the level of these people in the upper class. What is it then?

I am sure you have seen or heard of people who are not highly intellectual but are very successful. Do you know why? It is because they understand how to go about getting what they want, not through criminal activity; they did things the right way. They learned and understood the factors that would influence their purpose. They used their roadmap to navigate their way to get to their purpose to either stay there or grow from that purpose into another. They have the right mindset for success. They know how to find the people they need to talk to, to push their purpose forward. They were able to identify the market demand for their product or service and create an appetite for it. They addressed the red tapes. They used fear as a propeller to their success, unlike most people who cower and relax in their comfort zone. These highly successful people take the ridiculous risk that most people would not take. They do the extraordinary because they want to achieve the extraordinary which is why they get their rewards in high numbers.

What you need to know is that everything is **'FIGURE-OUT-ABLE'**. If you want it, you can get it if you know how. I can't tell you how in this book because I can't do that for the over 7 billion people on earth with different purposes. What I can tell you is that there is a process for how to achieve anything you want to, beyond any seeming obstacles. When you understand the order of how things work in life, by applying the steps in this book, then you would see opportunities not roadblocks. You will also need to learn and understand the dynamics of time in relation to your purpose. Study your environment, industry, or area of operation, not just within the geography you live, but that of other regions. Get to know people, and this means you have to put yourself out there by networking in the right circles. If you have to pay to be at certain events to meet someone who can play a part in your purpose, do it!

In October 2019, I attended the Federation of Awarding Bodies conference at Leicester, England when I got information that the CEO of an education awarding body that I wanted to partner with would be delivering a talk at the event. I bought my ticket for the event with the goal of meeting him. As soon as the event was over,

I walked up to Rob where he was talking to a bunch of people and introduced myself and said right away, "We need to talk." Looking at me in astonishment, we got talking. I told him what I had in mind and it turned out we have other common interests. Well, after a few minutes of talking, we scheduled to meet again more formally. We met again at a private members club in London, and today we are in a business partnership. If you want to meet someone of value who will be instrumental to your purpose, you can. You just have to raise your thought levels and actions to be in line with that goal in order to achieve it. You can't think big and act small, then expect to achieve big. You also have to dig into your pockets and spend money where necessary to achieve your purpose. If you are stingy with life, life will be stingy with you.

Everything about your 'being' has to be aligned with your purpose and this includes how you navigate yourself in the world to achieve it. This requires a great deal of effort on your part, self-discipline and sacrifice, which most people have a hard time committing to. It is the reason why so many are subject to the common order of things, and keeps many average, or worse below average, in life.

As you define your purpose, don't focus too much on the results, and get too excited about how successful it can be, but focus on the steps to get to the success you want. Too often, you have people celebrating success before it happens and bragging about it when they have some positive results and then you find them in the club, popping champagne. Yes, it is okay to celebrate little successes, but going overboard with it is self-defeating. The air of the world is currently filled with a lot of negative energy, and you could attract some form of negativity which kills your purpose before it fully matures. Imagine seeing Warren Buffet or Jeff Bezos in the club, popping champagne just because they made £1,000,000. They were busy working on getting to the high billions and any form of excessive recreation for that little success in relation to where they are now would have been self-defeating. **Their ambition becomes their recreation** which enables them to be more productive, including surrounding themselves with forward-thinking, high-impactful individuals that will propel them to optimal success. You need to have this same mental attitude to succeed. You have to know who-is-who in relation to your purpose and work with them. You will reduce costly mistakes and shorten the time it takes you to achieve your purpose.

Try This

1. Identify the factors you need to achieve your purpose.

2. Write down a minimum of 5 of these factors.

3. For each of these factors, write down the Who, Where, When and the How for each of them.

4. Link these factors and their associates to the relevant parts of your roadmap, as discussed in chapters 1 and 2.

5. Draw up an action log to track your progress daily.

V

Step Five: Know Your Economics

Life is economics, the natural system of profit and loss. This simply means some people will gain money and some people will lose money. In secondary school, I studied Home Economics as a subject. I didn't think I would make reference to it again or remember the principle of economics at that level, which was primarily centred on the basics of home management, including personal finance and the basics of saving money.

Economics is mainly about how money works whether at home, in business, in communities or countries of the world. It is the financial fuel, or liquidity, required to make things happen wherever you are in the world, and it can mean life and death for those who have it or don't have it.

You can't achieve anything significant in this world without money. Having a purposeful understanding of how money works makes you use it as fuel to achieve the things you want to in your personal life or business. The thing that most people are concerned about is how to get more money. I say more money because the price of consumer commodities or food does not stay the same due to that word we love to hate called 'INFLATION'. If you owned £1,000,000 in 2010 and did nothing to increase the value of your wealth, while still living the millionaire lifestyle, you'll most likely have run out of money by now. I once heard someone say, *"If you keep a thousand dollars in your drawer today and go to collect it a few years later, it is still going to be a thousand dollars"*. Worse thing is that the money would be devalued as a result of inflation just like when you drive a brand-new car out of the showroom and you take it back to sell it to the showroom, they won't buy it at the same value they sold it to you. This is the simple dynamics of economics that you need to know, because the inefficient use of money leads to problems and will affect your purpose.

Using money efficiently means that you have to

purposefully increase it according to the economies of the jurisdiction you live in. If you live in one economic jurisdiction and you want to do business in other parts of the world, or enjoy the finer things in life, then you have to increase your wealth to take into consideration the cost of things in the wider global economy. A millionaire in Nigeria is not automatically a millionaire in the United Kingdom. You have to create flows of income to fuel your life now and until you die. The income you create should be used for wealth creation, wealth planning, expenditure for yourself and your family, business investments, liabilities. This means you have to think your money in the long term. This goes for both men and women. The mistake most women make is to plan in the short term because they expect to be married and live off the income of their husbands, particularly in developing nations such as Africa, South and Central America, and Asia. The problem with this is that if, sadly, the marriage breaks down or the husband dies, women often struggle the most.

In Nigeria, for example, sadly you have places where the relatives of the deceased husband come in and take all the assets the man must have built up which makes life more difficult for the widow. Women ought to strongly consider long term wealth planning seriously as much as men do. It is just the right thing to do. On the flip side of that, men, get your will in place so that, if you die, your assets are protected and can keep taking care of your family. You will not cheat death by avoiding this seeming sensitive subject. It is part of knowing your Economics 101.

It is very clear that the reason multiple types of financial institutions exist all over the world is because 'money makes the world go round,' figuratively speaking. The years I spent working with financial institutions like Deutsche Bank, Euroclear, VISA, and Wealth Management firms like Jupiter Asset Management and Brewin Dolphin, revealed one thing in common with all of them: MONEY MANAGEMENT. No financial institution will exist if the product and service is not money related. They are responsible for managing other people's money for a fee. Through strict regulations, they offer you some sort of a guarantee to keep your money safely and even give you little interest in some cases. What happens when you put your money in the bank? It is not just there waiting for the day you come to collect.

Your money, along with that of others, is used to do business by the bank. This is one reason banks lead in the economies of the world.

You need to have this same mindset as these financial institutions and create ways to provide a service that will earn you other people's money, know how to use it and grow it. If you think that money, or having so much of it, is a sin, as some people think, then you have the wrong understanding of it. Remember, even Jesus paid his tax with money, which he miraculously got from the mouth of a fish; how rich do you think Jesus was? Financial misunderstanding leaves a lot of people in poverty or financial difficulty. Absorb this chapter and start to make changes if you need to. Money is not bad; it is a great protection for you and your family. You just need wisdom over it, as the Bible says in Ecclesiastes chapter 7 verse 12. I love this bit: *"...wisdom is a protection just as **money is a protection**, but the advantage of knowledge is this: Wisdom preserves the life of its owner."* Get your money wisdom right!

Falling on financial hard times, bad debt and bankruptcy is not a crime or something to be ashamed of as society would make you think. Consider bad debt as a rebalancing tool. They are tools I have used myself to create a rebalancing of my financial trajectory. Those who looked upon me with distaste then, I look at them with pity now because they are still caught up working for other people as employees, while I am an employer. Never let common limiting beliefs about money, or the challenges of money, hold you back from taking the necessary action you need to achieve your purpose. Take the necessary actions that do not require money; define your purpose, create your roadmap with the goals you need to get you to your purpose, create the attention you need directed at the people that will either facilitate your idea or who will buy your idea. There is a lot you can do, with little or no money, to achieve your purpose. Start something to get something back in return.

Okay, money does not make the world go round *literally*, but people with great innovative ideas do, and ideas cost nothing. There are many ways to go about getting money. You can teach what you know if it solves a problem or creates some kind of satisfaction for an intended audience. Your idea, products or services provides a solution. Use it to solve problems for people or business owners for a fee. This is called consulting; the word is not reserved for big companies only. You can partner with someone who loves your idea who's got the money – you bring the idea; they bring the money. You may qualify for government grants, that may exist where you live, to support your business idea.

When you start to generate the revenue from your implemented idea, you need to support your business by investing it back in your business to increase the quality and quantity of your products and services. Keep this in mind; don't expect to start a business and become an overnight success. You need to allow your business to get the traction it needs with some promotion and marketing effort from you. If your aspirations are long term, then you need to give your business a minimum of 3 years for the 'cement' to set before real growth begins. Keep records. Book-keeping is vital so you know what is coming in and going out. If you're not great at doing this yourself, hire a freelance accountant to do it for you and ensure that they keep your books right with the tax man. It is your responsibility to pay any due taxes.

The purpose of this chapter is to share with you some

of the basic principles of money that we often don't get taught by our parents or at school. It should not come to you as a surprise that there are people who study money-related courses at university or work in financial institutions that do poorly when it comes to getting and managing money. Don't be too hard on them. It is because the fundamentals of what they were taught lack the practical elements for real life. It took me some time to learn and know about money properly. Even at that, I am still learning as our economy changes. I hope that you find value, not just in this chapter but in the whole book. My goal is to help as many people as possible achieve their purpose using the steps I have outlined in this book.

Remember this vital information:

• Financial crises will always happen for as long as we have financial institutions. Don't panic. Be prepared and expect one on an average of every 7 to 15 years. This might be triggered by an event that is directly or indirectly related to financial services companies, but it leads to the same outcome – economic crisis, with some sort of financial system rebalancing exercises undertaken by financial institutions. This is a reality that is known by a few. It is how the world works. Knowing this could help you prepare for the future.

• Bad debt, including bankruptcy, is a financial rebalancing tool and, if used correctly, could get you back into a good financial position. Use bad debt as a tool where necessary to rebalance your finances. If big corporations can use it, why can't you?

• If you have a business, you are not your business. It is a separate entity from you, and you need to treat your business finance as separate from your personal finance.

• Money is a universal language, but currency is like the weight plates on a barbell; it has weight in varying degrees.

• Use your money to fortify yourself first, so you can be around longer to fortify others with your wealth.

• Instead of keeping money in the bank for it to grow, why don't you use it to create products or services that will give you more than the banks will? When you look at the interest on most savings accounts, it is clear you can't save your money to achieve financial freedom. All the savings might be stolen from you by death. Use it while you can.

Try This

1. Evaluate your personal economy by carrying out an income and expenditure analysis. What is coming in? What is going out? Is your income sufficient to cover all your expenditure? If there is anything unnecessary that is an expenditure and provides no value, stop spending on it.

2. Carry out the above income and expenditure analysis on your business, if you have one. This is usually more complex for businesses. Your accountant will be able to help you.

3. Sell your expertise as a personal brand. This can open up many revenue doors for you.

VI

Step Six: Use Your Failure Wisely

We all have them, but the big difference is how you understand and use your own failure. You will have multiple failures in life; personal, family, work or business, and it doesn't matter because it is okay to have them. You have these failures right from the day you are born. How is that so? When you are born, often times you try to repeat patterns you formed while you were in your mother's womb and you fail because the environment you spent the last nine months in changed due to an event out of your control. Birth! You don't recognise this new environment and you are unfamiliar with how to operate in this new place. This makes you start to cry. This is the beginning of your first failures; from trying to walk and falling on your bum as a toddler to what we call serious mistakes in adulthood. Keep this in mind, failure happens accordingly. You cannot have a failure that is meant for someone else. Every failure that happens to you is meant for you because the elements involved in bringing that failure about involved an action or inaction from you. When it happens, don't moan and say, "why me?". It won't change the situation.

What is important is what you do when failure happens, how you react to it, how quickly you can turn the failure around to achieve a best-case outcome. It is worth noting that failure is not all bad. As a matter of fact, it can present you with an opportunity. When failure happens, instead of beating yourself up about it, analyse the failure to see what it is telling you. Every bit of information about that failure is data that is available to you, which you can use to do so much.

Failure gives you both good, bad, useful and worthless data. Not all good data is useful, just as not all bad data is worthless. A data point in a failure can be good-to-know information but may not serve you any rewarding purpose, whereas a bad data point may be an identified opportunity which leads to reward if you can turn it around.

For example, let's say you have a difficulty with speaking publicly and you lack the confidence to speak with people you are not familiar with. Even when demeaned and bullied, you are scared to speak your mind. When asked why you don't stand up for yourself, you brush it off and avoid confronting your fears. That is a bad data point which presents you with an opportunity, an opportunity to have an inward look into yourself to find out the reason that led you to being that way. Once you have done that self-assessment, you have identified the incident that led to your lack of confidence, which could be things like being shouted at by your parents constantly when you were a child, being bullied in school, or the actual fear of doing or saying the wrong things. Whatever it is, once you address the source of that bad data point through taking the time to understand it, then performing the exercises to build your confidence and putting it into practice, you begin to find that your confidence grows. You are bolder, respond to people without fear, your personal life improves, your professional life improves. You may even become a paid public speaker. In this sequence, you have taken a bad data point from a failure in your life, identified the opportunity within it, and turned that opportunity to a reward you never had. You have an added value to you and increased your self-worth and net worth.

The point of this exercise is to show you that failure is not absolute. It is in times of failure that I have identified some of the best opportunities that I am benefiting from today. Try this exercise on any failure, both past and present, that you have experienced in your life to find out what opportunities exist in them. You cannot be an absolute failure – period!

See failures as experiments. The COVID-19 vaccine became rewarding after many experiments before it was put to production and then administered to people. Change your mindset and turn your failures into experiments. When you see failure that way, you no longer see bad in them, but potential opportunities. To do so, you will have to be bold and not recoil into yourself when failure happens. Shying away from your failure prevents you from taking pragmatic action to address it and could increase the time it takes you to recover from a failure. Worse still, it could prevent you from getting the rewards that can come from the opportunities in failure.

Many of the beliefs about failure today come from cultures or traditions, religion, social trends or how the corporate world over-accentuates failure. What you may not know is that, while failure may be creating fear, and limiting or slowing down your progress, there may be people who are benefiting from your failure and creating reward for themselves. *'One man or woman's poison is another man or woman's meat.'* If anyone should benefit from your failure, it should be you.

Maintain a positive attitude by visualising the future you want beyond the failure. Take little actions that require no cost. Talk only to people who will fuel you with positive feelings, and don't forget to get out and go for a walk when your head feels clouded. The effects of fresh air on your brain can work wonders, as well as just being out of your home and observing nature. It may sound so simple, but it is the simplest things that create massive results and can spark a change for the better in your life. There is no magic in life, but actions that lead to outcome.

I mentioned earlier how religion and tradition can influence the way you view failure. Do you wonder how? I feel it is vital to emphasise this point because sometimes, when bad things happen, you hear people refer to things like a generational curse as the reason for failures that happen in their lives, or that their ancestor in the spirit world has something to do with it. These are lies. What you need to know is that you, or your immediate environment, can greatly influence you for good or for bad. This can be responsible for the failures you have, directly or indirectly. That also means you have the power to transform yourself, to change deeply engrained limiting forces that are holding you back from the success you want. It is not going to be easy, but with great effort, you can change the habit of being the person you are now to become the person you want to be, with the right information and consistent work.

In relation to the role religion plays in how you view failure, particularly in Christendom churches, many are made to believe, by their leaders, that they either have a demon or are not paying enough money contribution to the church. This is the reason you experience failures in your life and are therefore deprived of material blessings from God. What is interesting about this is that many of the followers are highly educated and hold high positions in companies, not to mention the many poor people, exploited because they look to these religious leaders as their saviour. The truth is that, if you want to overcome any challenges or failure, you have to work hard to get past them. It's been said many times over, 'no pain, no gain,' so trying to take these religious shortcuts will not bring you reward. You will not fly in that private jet your pastor flies in.

What is remarkable about you is that your brain's ability to change and adapt, known as plasticity of the brain or neuroplasticity, is so powerful that, if powered right with the correct information backed by solid actions, you will override strongly entrenched idiosyncrasies that have been formed over a period of time, even decades, through repeated subconscious and conscious patterns. You will need to exert yourself really hard to overcome them and you can be assured that success is at the other end of it. As I have already shown you, there is treasure in every failure. You just have to find it.

One of the things I am successful at is finding treasures in failures, whether in mine or the people who work with me. I convert failures into treasures that bring smiles to faces. That is for me the greatest reward. The joy of helping people when there seems to be no way out. When you have the power of thought beyond the ordinary, and are willing to welcome change, then failures become treasures.

Great successes have come from failures. Often, you have to get it wrong before you can get it right and it does not matter how many times you fail. What matters is that you keep getting up until you achieve your purpose. This resilient mindset in times of failure will be a strong determinant for how you recover. Keep this in mind; *a failure is a disguised opportunity waiting to be exploited for the reward it gives.*

Try This

1. Write down all the failures you have had in your life that you can remember since you were sixteen until now.

2. Analyse the details of these failures to the best of your ability.

    a. What caused or triggered the failure?

b. What was happening three months before the incident took place?

c. What was your state of mind?

d. Who were the actors or actresses in the failure?

e. Are they still present in your life?

f. When did the failure happen?

g. Did you resolve the failure?

h. How did you resolve it?

i. What value did you get from the failure?

j. If the failure is not yet resolved, is it because you decided to just live with it?

k. What can you do now to resolve a lifelong failure?

l. What are the things you learned about yourself, the failure, and its impact on the people it affected?

3. Analyse all data you have put together about the failures.

4. An opportunity is the potential for a reward from an activity undertaken. What opportunity do you see that you could use to bring reward to you and others now?

5. Once you have identified an opportunity from a failure you have had, take the first step now to work

on getting the reward presented in the opportunity. Maintain your progress towards the reward with continuous action until you can quantify it.

6. Be grateful for your failures. If you are ashamed of your failures, then the reward your failures offer will be ashamed of you too.

VII

Step Seven: Be Conscious of Your Spiritual Need

I believe this is the beginning of true happiness and the true sense of what purpose really is, the point when you experience the state of flow that is in sync with universal purpose. It is interesting to watch how a vast number of people go through life without knowing that there is symbiosis of self that needs to be formed with universal purpose.

You have your physical self that craves the desires of what the flesh wants and needs, food, sex, assets, security, money and much more. Then you have your emotional self and mental self. How do you unite these various selves in harmony so that your purpose in life can be more meaningful and satisfactory? Your spiritual self. This is your uniting force that is instinctively built in all humans whether you like it or not, or know it or not. It is there, and the greatest evidence of this is the quest all humans are on in the finding of meaning to life.

How do you use it? Whatever you do in life whether in business, career, being a parent, husband, wife, student, politician, leader, man, woman, boy or girl, you need to be conscious of this instinctive spiritual need, and feed it just like you feed your other selves. The way I feed my spiritual need will be different from how you feed yours or not. And the thing is, even if you are not actively or consciously feeding your spiritual hunger, you are feeding it with something. So, you need to be conscious about it in order for your life, and everything you do with it, to be in harmony with your purpose.

You may have heard some people, who are very successful from a monetary point of view, say that they feel empty even though they have a lot of money. That is a symptom of someone who is not feeding their spiritual need consciously, or they are feeding it with something that does not create harmony with universal purpose.

Where do you find true internal peace? Why is this so

important? It is because it affects your productivity and can resonate in your immediate environment; that is, delocalisation from, ultimately, universal purpose. It will be like being in a group of people and not being seen or heard or, even worse, being there and feeling you are not there. Ever had that feeling? As much as this is vital for individuals, it is more vital for businesses and organisations with small to large teams. This goes beyond having a Human Resources department in a company as the status quo to take care of the people element. It requires someone who understands the value of spirituality in an organisation and the effect it has on business in order to efficiently direct the resources of the humans that work there in a way that will not only fulfil their targets and goals, but also give meaning to the lives of these humans beyond the exploitation of the resources they provide.

It is important to know that, when you start to interact with people, you interact with their spiritual state as well, and that can influence you for the good or the bad. Have you ever been with someone or at a place where the energy just doesn't feel right, even though nothing bad around seems to be happening? That is a symptom of the spiritual nature of that environment. Most energies in an environment, or from people, are not right for you or the achievement of your purpose.

My attempt here is not to go deep into what spirituality or true spirituality is and should be for you. Everyone needs to find it. I have found mine. My duty is to tell you that you need to be conscious about it and feed it with the right spiritual food because there is so much noise about spirituality out there right now that is being pumped into the minds of people. This creates confusion which is super distracting and keeps you unhinged from universal harmony. Be in control of what you absorb. Do your own research using reliable, timeless and tested information.

One thing needs to be consistent for universal harmony to exist – the information we take in. As a community of people, regardless of where you come from on this planet, for universal harmony to exist amongst us and to be hinged on to the wider universal purpose, we need to absorb information that is consistent with that purpose. Knowledge and wisdom exist in numerous forms. Some people like to get their wisdom from gurus, yogis, philosophers, religious leaders or other influencers. It is your personal choice to get your information from where you wish but it is more important that you check the message these people are transmitting to you. What I find crazy about this is that many followers of these people, in most cases, do not think for themselves or carry out simple research to test the information they take in from the people they blindly worship. You owe it to yourself to validate the information you consume.

I hope the message in this book helps you quieten down the noise so you can give mindful and meaningful thought to your purpose. This will help you to be more conscious about your true spiritual need. You will become more aligned with universal purpose in order for you to be entwined with universal harmony and achieve your purpose successfully.

Try This

If you have defined your purpose, or are working on it now, write down the following and review as your purpose evolves:

1. How does your purpose affect you?

2. How does if impact your family?

3. How does it affect the way you learn and teach others through your purpose (Education)?

4. How does your work or business fulfil your purpose?

5. What is the impact of your purpose in your community?

6. What is the impact of your purpose on the economy?

7. What is the impact of your purpose on your country?

8. How does your purpose have an impact on the way you transact with the earth?

The Conclusion of This Book is the Beginning of Your Journey to Achieving Your Purpose

Thank you for taking the time to purchase and read this book. It is my sincerest effort to share something so valuable with you that I hope will have a positive impact in your life on as many levels as possible.

Purpose begets purpose. By that I mean that your purpose, my purpose and your purpose, everyone's purpose, plugs into a much grander unifying purpose. Let's find it together. No one's purpose is independent of another's. The success of one person is not the success of everyone. We all need to succeed collectively and by opening up my purpose to you, I help you achieve yours and I urge you to open up your purpose to the right people. By doing this, we contribute to the greater good of the world.

I want this book to reach millions of people by 2025 to help as many as possible to achieve their purpose. Let everyone you come in contact with know about this book.

About the Author

Chizubel Egwudo is a Risk Strategist who has advised and enabled some of the top executives of FTSE100 companies and business owners, helping them achieve their purpose. He delivers business lectures at institutions of higher education and trains company executives and professionals in the art of applying appropriate risk strategies for success.

Chizubel is an Entrepreneur and Business Coach. He is the pioneer and founder of The Risk of You as a company and as a new movement that advocates the power of risk in personal and business life. He is also the CEO of School of Risk, a learning and development company devoted to the education of risk in all sectors of work.

Mr Egwudo is a trained Neuro Linguistic Practitioner under the tutelage of Mr Richard Bandler – cofounder of NLP. Chizubel is a rising star in his own unique way of helping leaders gain reward from their endeavours. He does this through consultations, advisory and bespoke coaching.

He shares his passion of inspiring, mentoring and developing people to overcome strongly entrenched fears or failure by presenting them with the rewards possible and gives them the steps to rise successfully.

Printed in Great Britain
by Amazon